Red Pandas

Curious Kids Press

Red Pandas

The Red Panda is a cute fluffy critter. It is a cousin to the Giant Panda. However, this animal does not really look like a bear. The Red Panda is also called, the Lesser Panda, the Red Cat-Bear and the Fire Fox. Are you ready to take a journey into the Red Panda world? Get ready because we are going to discover all sorts of cool and interesting facts. Some may even amaze your friends. Lets read on...

Where in the World?

Did you know the Red Panda lives in forests made of bamboo? It's true! It can be found in some provinces of China. It also hangs around in the foothills of the tall mountain range called the, Himalayas. This area is very cold. Read on to discover how the Red Panda handles the weather.

The Body of a Panda

Did you know the Red Panda has thick fur? Its beautiful coat helps keep it warm. It has deep red-colored fur on its body and black fur on its legs. It has small rounded white ears on top of its head. Its nose and small eyes are black. The Red Panda has a short muzzle with white fur on its face.

The Size of the Red Panda

Did you know the Red Panda is quite small? If you have ever seen a raccoon, then you will know about how big the Red Panda is. It can measure around 42 inches long (106 centimeters); this includes its tail. Most Red Pandas can weigh about 14 pounds (6.3 kilograms). This is a lot smaller than most bears!

The Red Panda's Tail

Did you know Red Pandas use their tails to keep warm? Red Pandas have long bushy tails with dark red rings around it. They will curl their tail around their body to keep warm in the winter. Their tail also helps them keep their balance while they climb around in the trees.

The Red Panda's Feet

Did you know the Red Panda has a thumb? Like a panda bear, the Red Panda has a thumb-like appendage. It uses this special thumb to grasp onto the bamboo. The Red Panda also uses this extra digit to climb trees. The bottom of this animal's feet is also covered in fur. This not only keeps it warm, but stops it from slipping on the wet branches.

What a Red Panda Eats

Did you know the Red Panda likes to eat lots of different foods? Red Pandas eat mostly bamboo leaves and the new shoots. But they also like to eat berries, blossoms, bird eggs, plants, mushrooms, lichen, maple and mulberry leaves, as well some tree bark. This mammal spends a lot of its time looking for food.

The Not-So-Social Red Panda

Did you know the Red Panda likes to be alone?
It will also defend its territory from other Red
Pandas. The only time the Red Panda isn't
alone is during mating season. The Red Panda
is mostly active at night and will spend the day
sleeping. To sleep it will find a hollow in a tree,
or stretch out on a long branch.

Red Panda Talk

Did you know the Red Panda can communicate? Red Panda's are mostly silent animals. But they will make a twittering, tweeting and whistling sound. These sound more like a bird, than a bear. They will also scent mark their territory. This is done with urine and lets the other Red Pandas know this part if the woods is taken.

The Red Panda as Prey

Did you know the Red Panda is still hunted by humans? This animal is poached by humans for its fur. Loss of its natural home is also a threat to the Red Panda. This animal is also hunted by the snow leopard and the marten. If in danger, the Red Panda will climb a tree to escape.

The Red Panda Mom

Did you know the Red Panda mom will carry her young for 134 days? She will give birth from mid-June to late July. Mom Red Panda will build a nest in a hollow of a tree. She uses brushwood, grass and leaves to make her nest warm and cozy.

The Baby Red Panda

Did you know the baby **Red Panda** will stay in the nest for 3 months? **Newborn** cubs are born blind and deaf. Each one will weigh around 110 to 130 grams (3.9 to 4.6 ounces). There can be up to four cubs in a litter. After about 18 days the cubs will open their eyes.

Life of a Red Panda

Did you know Red Pandas are endangered? There are less than 10,000 adult Red Pandas left in the wild today. These animals are now protected from being hunted. A healthy Red Panda can live to be from 8 to 10 years-old in the wild. However, in captivity (like a zoo) this animal can live to be 15 years-old.

The Giant Panda

Giant Panda's are a cousin to the Red Panda. These bears can be found in and around the same area as the Red Panda. This big bear is white with black patches on its face and body. They eat nothing but bamboo. The Giant Panda also has a "thumb." This helps it to grasp the bamboo and to climb trees.

Raccoon

Since the Red Panda resembles a raccoon, here is a bit about this cool animal. Raccoons are found in North American. They have a black "mask" around their eyes. Their front paws resemble hands. The raccoon is very smart and is known to get into people's garbage. It is greyish in color with black rings around its tail.

Quiz

Question 1: What famous mountain range can the Red Panda be found around?

Answer 1: The Himalayans

Question 2: What color is the Red Panda's fur?

Answer 2: Mostly red with black legs and white markings on its face

Question 3: What is special about the Red Panda's feet?

Answer 3: It has a thumb-like appendage and the bottoms are covered in fur

Question 4: Does the Red Panda like to live alone or with other Red Pandas?

Answer 4: It prefers to live alone

Question 5: Where does the mother Red Panda have her young?

Answer 5: In a nest in the hollow of a tree

Thank you for checking out another title from Curious Kids Press! Make sure to search "Curious Kids Press" on Amazon.com for many other great books.

Made in the USA
Lexington, KY
08 December 2016